CW00404315

101 HILARIOUS DUMB BLONDE JOKES

Laugh Out Loud With These Funny Blondes Jokes: Even Your Blonde Friend Will LOL! (WITH 30+ PICTURES)

Johnny Riddle

Table of Contents

INTRODUCTION

First joke: Q: How do you keep a blonde girl occupied?

A: Give her a piece of paper, and write "flip it" on both sides!

Or how about this one:

Q: What did the blonde girl say, when the doctor congratulated her with her pregnancy?

A: "Gee, I wonder: is it mine?"

Thank you for picking up a copy of '*101 Hilarious Dumb Blonde Jokes.*'

Are you ready to crack up about these funny blonde jokes?

<u>Laughter is good</u> for you!

You probably already knew that. I mean, who doesn't feel good when they laugh, right?

But did you know that laughter is associated with all these health benefits?

Laughter:

- relaxes your body
- boosts your immune system
- triggers the release of feel-good hormones, such as endorphins
- protects your heart

When you're reading or telling these jokes, you're *also* working on your health!

Sounds good, right?

If you're looking for a good laugh, you've come to the right place!

This book is jam-packed with:

- 100+ hilarious clean jokes, and
- 30+ funny illustrations

that everyone will love.

So, I hope you – and your family or friends – are ready to *roar with laughter.* **let's get started with the first joke!**

101 HILARIOUS DUMB BLONDE JOKES

1.

One day, a blonde went to a pizzeria and ordered a pizza. The waitress asked if she wanted her pizza cut into six or twelve pieces. "Six", the blonde replied, "You don't really think I eat twelve, do you?!"

2.

A brunette, a blonde and a redhead got lost on a hike in the desert. After walking for hours, they stumbled upon a lamp, half buried in the sand. As they rubbed it, a genie popped out! He said: "I will grant each of you one wish."

Excited, the redhead said: "I wish to be back home". And poof!, the next moment she found herself back in her home.

Next, the brunette said: "I wish to be with my family, at home". Poof!, she was also transported back home immediately, surrounded by her loved ones.

Then the blonde said: "I wish my friends were here."

3.

When going for a walk, two blondes fell down a deep and dark hole. After checking in with each other, one blonde said, "It is really dark in here, right?"

To which the other blonde replied, "I honestly don't know, I can't see anything!"

4.

Q: Why can't a blonde dial 911?

A: She gets stuck trying to find eleven.

5.

A brunette, a blonde and a redhead found themselves trapped on an island. They decided their only option for survival was to try to swim to the nearest shore, 40 miles away.

The brunette went first. She swam 20 miles, but then was so exhausted that she drowned.

The redhead swam 25 miles, but then also drowned.

Finally, the blonde swam 35 miles, but when she got tired, she swam back.

6.

Q: How do you confuse a blonde?

A: Tell to her sit in the corner, after putting her in a circle.

7.

In the 19th century, a brunette, a redhead, and a blonde are on death row. They are about to be executed by a firing squad.

The guards start with the brunette. When she is asked if she has any last request, she says: "No." The guards point their guns at her, when the captain shouts: "Ready. Aim..." But then, suddenly, the brunette screams, "Tornado!" As everyone is freaking out, looking for shelter, the brunette escapes.

Next, the guards put the redhead against the wall. She also says "No" when she is asked if she has a last request. The captain shouts "Ready. Aim...", and then the redhead yells "Earthquake!" Again, the guards are freaking out, running all over the place, and in the commotion, the redhead is able to escape.

All this time, the blonde has been paying attention. And she knows what to do now. The guards put her against the wall. When asked, she says she doesn't have any final requests. The captain says:

bring her forward, and the executioner asks if she has any last requests. She also says no, and the executioner yells "Ready. Aim..."

The blonde screams, "Fire!"

8.

Q: Why does it take hours to build a blonde snowman?

A: Because, unlike a regular snowman, you need to hollow out the head.

9.

One day, three blondes went on a walk in the woods. After a few hours, they spotted some tracks.

The first blonde said, excited: "Look, it's bear tracks!"

The second blonde replied, "No, those are deer tracks".

Before the third blonde was able to share her opinion, the blondes got hit by a train...

10.

Q: What do you call a blonde with a high IQ?

A: A golden retriever.

11.

200 blondes came together in Los Angeles, intent on showing the people that blondes can be smart. They said to the people passing by: "You can ask us anything you want! Anything. We will show you we're smarter than you think."

A passer-by took them up on their offer. He chose one blonde from the group, and asked her the first question, surrounded by the other 199 blondes.

"Who is the president of the United States?" The blonde said: "Michael Jordan?" "I'm sorry, that's not correct," the man said. The other blondes then chanted: "Please let her try again!"

The man then asked: "What's the color of grass?" The blonde said: "Blue?". "No, it's green", the man responded. The group of blondes began shouting again: "Let her try again!"

The man was running out of patience, and said: "I'll give her one more chance, but this is the last question! How many corners does a triangle have?" The blonde responded: "Three?"

"Please let her try again!", the group of blondes yelled...

12.

Q: What does a blonde girl do when her laptop freezes?

A: She puts in the microwave!

13.

Q: Why does a blonde carry a ladder when she goes to the bar?

A: Her friend told her cocktails were on the house.

14.

A guy took a blonde girl on a date. She had told him she had never been to a football game, so he got 2 tickets for the game. To impress her, he had gotten two seats right behind the home team's bench.

When the game was over, he asked her: "How did you like the game?"

"Thanks for taking me here, I really liked it," she replied. "I liked the big muscles and tight pants. But there's one thing I couldn't figure out: why they were they all killing each other over a measly 25 cents?"

Dumbfounded, the guy asked, "Huh, I don't understand: what do you mean?"

"Well, at the beginning of the game, they ref flipped a coin, one team got it, and then for the rest of the game, all they kept yelling was, 'Get the quarterback! Get that quarterback!' I was like: take it easy guys, it's only 25 cents!"

15.

A blonde girl was having a coffee with her brunette friend when she started complaining about her boyfriend's dandruff problem. The brunette said: "Well, just give him Head and Shoulders."

To which the blonde girl responded, "How do you give shoulders?"

16.

Q: What do a blonde girl and a beer bottle have in common?

A: Both are empty from the neck up.

17.

Q: A blonde and a brunette decided they wanted to commit suicide by jumping from a skyscraper. Who jumped first?

A: The brunette. The blonde girl first had to ask for directions.

18.

Q: What can strike a blonde girl without her even realizing it?

A: A thought.

19.

Q: What do you call a blonde girl holding a red balloon?

A: Siamese twins.

20.

Q: Why shouldn't you give a blonde a coffee break at work?

A: It would take too long to retrain her.

21.

Over drinks, a blonde girl was discussing the blind date she had a few days ago to a male friend. "We had dinner, it was great" she said, "next, he wanted to come back with me to my house. However, I politely refused. I told him my mom would be very worried if I did anything like that." "That was a smart move from you," her male friend said. "So, what happened next?"

"Well, he was a bit pushy, and I kept refusing," the blonde said. "You didn't give in though, did you?" her male friend asked. "No, of course not! In the end, we agreed to go to his house. I was like, let his mother worry..."

22.

Q: How would you be able to tell if a brunette is actually a blonde girl who died her hair?

A: When she falls over a cordless phone!

23.

Q: Why does a blonde girl wear her hair up?

A: So she can catch everything that goes over her head!

24.

Q: What would you call 10 blonde girls standing close to each other, ear to ear?

A: A wind tunnel!

25.

Q: Why do blonde girls put lipstick on their foreheads?

A: Because they are trying to make up their minds.

26.

One evening, a guy wanted to go to bed, when he found his bed sheets covered with sugar.

Baffled, he yelled at his blonde girlfriend: "Why on earth would you do that?!"

To which the blonde replied: "Because I want us to have sweet dreams, baby. "

27.

Q: Why was the blonde girl talking into an envelope at the post office?

A: She wanted to send a voicemail!

28.

Two sisters, a blonde and a brunette, inherited a ranch from their parents. Unfortunately, they have just lost their bull. The sisters need to buy another one, but only have $400 between the both of them. The brunette tells her blonde sister, "I will go into town, to the cow market, and see if I can find us a new bull for less than $400. I will send you a telegram if I can, OK?"

So, the brunette goes to the cow market, walks around, and she's in luck: she finds a good-looking bull for $399. However, this means she only has one dollar left. Moreover, at the telegraph office, she learns that it costs $1 per word to send a telegram.

She takes a few moments to figure out how to tell her blonde sister to bring the truck and trailer from the ranch.

Finally, she knows what to do. She tells the telegraph operator: send her the word "comfortable."

Puzzled, the operator asks, "I don't understand: how will your sister know to come with the truck and trailer from just this word?"

The brunette replies, "My sis is a blonde, so she reads really slow: 'Come for ta bull...'"

29.

A blonde got home, all excited. "I got a compliment on my driving today", she told her boyfriend. "How so?", he asked.

"Somebody left a note on my windshield", the blonde replied, "You know what it said? 'Parking Fine'!"

30.

On her first solo flight, a blonde girl crashed her helicopter.

When asked by a police officer what happened, she said: "I was cold, so I decided to turn off the fan."

31.

Q: What should you do in case a blonde girl throws a pin in your direction?

A: Run, Forest, Run, she has a grenade in her hand!

32.

A police car pulled over a blonde girl, because she was speeding in a residential zone. It just so happened that the female police officer was also blonde. She tapped on the window, and said: "Please show me your driver's license, mam."

The blonde driver searched frantically, in her purse and elsewhere in the car. Finally, she asked the blonde cop, "Can you tell me what a driver's license looks like?' Annoyed by so much stupidity, the blonde policewoman said, "Don't try to be smart with me!, it has your photo on it!"

The blonde driver searched her purse again. This time, she found a small mirror down at the bottom. She took it out and held it up to her face. "Aha! This must be my driver's license", she said. She handed it to the cop.

The blonde policewoman looked in the mirror, gave it back to the blonde driver and said, "Thank you, you are free to go. Why didn't you tell me you were a police officer too? Then we could have avoided all of this!"

33.

Q: Why did the M&M factory decide to fire their blonde employee?

A: Because she kept throwing away all the W's!

34.

A blonde girl was watching the evening news. One of items was about a serial killer, the news anchor said he was on the loose.

So, the blonde wasted no time. She rushed into the kitchen, grabbed all her cereal from the shelves and brought it down to the basement.

"Don't worry, cereal, no one can kill you here!", she said.

35.

Once upon a time, there was a blonde who was totally fed up with all the dumb blonde jokes. She decided she would take an evening to memorize all the state capitals.

When she went back in the office the next day, one of her colleagues started telling a blonde joke. "Now is the right time", she said to herself.

She interrupted him and said, "I've had it up to here with these dumb blonde jokes. This blonde here did some studying last night, and I'm pretty sure I did something none of you can do: I memorized all the state capitals." One of her male colleagues said, "Really? I don't believe you. Let's test that. What is the capital of Nevada?"

"N," the blonde answered.

36.

Eleven people are hanging onto a rope that comes down from an airplane. One of them is a redhead, the other ten are blonde.

The rope is about to break, so they all decide that one person has to take one for the team: she should get off the rope, because if no one does, the rope will break and everyone will fall to their death.

They can't agree on who should go, though. Ultimately, the redhead delivers a very touching speech, ending with the words, "I'll let go off the rope."

The ten blondes, all very moved by the redhead's speech, start to applaud.

Problem solved.

37.

One day, a science teacher told his high school class, "Oxygen is a must for breathing and staying alive. It was first discovered in the year 1773."

A blonde student responded, "Omg, I am so happy I was born after 1773 then! Otherwise I would have died instantly."

38.

Q: What did the blonde girl say when she opened a box of Cheerios?

A: "Yes, donut seeds!"

39.

A redhead visits the doctor's office. She says: "My body hurts, wherever I touch it. Can you help?"

"That's impossible," the doctor replies. "Can you show me?"

The redhead takes her finger, presses on her knee, and screams in agony. Then, she pushes her shoulder and screams again. Same with her elbow. It goes on and on; wherever she touched her body, she screams with pain.

Finally, the doctor says, "That's enough. You are not really a redhead now, are you?" She replies, "Actually no, I'm naturally blonde. I dyed my hair red, how did you know?"

"Because your finger is broken," the doctor said.

40.

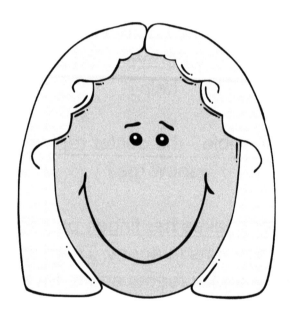

Q: Why did the blonde tip-toe when she walked near the medicine cabinet?

A: Because she was afraid of waking up the sleeping pills!

41.

A guy was about to go on a long drive to his parents, to celebrate Thanksgiving. Before hitting the road, he wanted to make sure the car was in good condition.

He asked his blonde girlfriend to stand outside and check if the blinker worked.

As he turned it on, she said, "Yes, No, Yes, No, Yes..."

42.

Q: Why do blonde girls leave empty beer bottles in their fridge?

A: In case they have friends come over that don't drink!

43.

Two blondes found themselves stuck in an elevator.

While one blonde started to cry, the other, more assertive, one started to yell, "Help, please help!"

Then, the crying blonde had a better idea, "Let's shout together?" "Good plan," said the other blonde. "Together! TOGETHER!"

44.

A blonde goes into a nearby Walmart to buy a TV. She asks the clerk: "Can I have that TV in the corner?" The clerk looks at her and says: "Sorry mam, I don't serve blondes."

Frustrated, she goes back home and dyes her hair red.

She returns the next day, asks the clerk the same thing, but again, the clerk said: "We don't serve blondes."

Even more upset, the blonde decides to give it one more try. This time, she dyes her hair brown. Surely, she'll be able to buy the TV this time, there are so many brunettes!

To increase her changes, when she gets back to Walmart, she approaches a different clerk. Again, she points to the TV she wants to buy.

To her astonishment, this clerk also says: "We do not sell to blondes."

The blonde, furious, asked the clerk, "What makes you think I'm a blonde, can't you see I'm a brunette?!"

To which the clerk replied: "You thought you could fool me? That's not a TV, it's a microwave!"

45.

One day, a blonde woman decided to hire herself out as a handyman-type. She was down on her luck, after buying air at a real bargain, and now she wanted to earn some extra cash. She felt she would have the best chance of getting hired if she would start going door-to-door in a wealthy neighborhood. She knocked on the door of the first house, and a man opened. She explained what she came to do, and asked: "Do you have a job for me?"

"Well, my porch needs to be painted again. How much would you charge for that?", the man said.

The blonde said, "I can do it for $60."

The man agreed: "The pain, ladders, and anything else you may need are all in the garage."

The man's wife had overheard the conversation, inside the house. When the man had closed the door, she asked: "Do you think she realizes that the porch goes all the way around the house?" "She should," the man said, "She was *standing* on the porch, after all, wasn't she?"

Only 30 minutes later, the blonde knocked on the door, asking for her money. "Huh, are you finished already?" the man asked, skeptically.

"Yes," the blonde replied, "and I even had some paint left over, so I gave it two coats." "That's really impressive", the man said to himself, as he reached in his pocket to give her the $60.

"Oh, one more thing," the blonde added, "I guess you didn't realize, but that's not a Porch. It's a Ferrari."

46.

A blonde is stopped for speeding. The police officer walks up to her car and asks for her driver's license.

"Seriously?", she replied, "Can't you guys get your act together? Just yesterday one of your colleagues took away my license. How do you expect me to show it to you today?"

47.

Did you hear about the blonde that got excited?
She finished a jigsaw puzzle in six months,
when the box said, "two to four years."

48.

Q: Why does a blonde girl put her iPad in a blender?

A: She wants to make apple juice!

49.

One evening, a blonde is watching the 6 o'clock news with her boyfriend, when the news anchor says, "6 Brazilian men have died in a parachute accident."

The next moment, the blonde starts sobbing uncontrollably, exclaiming: "That's terrible!"

Her boyfriend, confused, replies, "I agree, sweetie. But then again: they were parachuting. There is always a risk involved with extreme sports like that."

After a few more minutes, the blonde, still crying, says, "Sweetie, tell me: how many is a Brazilian?"

50.

Tired of the countless blonde jokes she hears all the time, a blonde decides enough is enough and dyes her hair black. Since she has the weekend off, she steps into her car to go for a drive in the country. After a few hours, a shepherd herding his sheep across the road catches her attention.

"Hello, shepherd," she says, "I have a proposal: if I guess how many sheep you have here, can I keep one?" The shepherd agrees thinks about it for a few seconds, but then agrees. She says: "246!"

The shepherd is stunned: "That's correct!"

Since he is a man of his word, he lets her to pick a sheep. "I will take this one," she says with a smile on her face. "He looks so cute!"

Then, the shepherd replies: "Hey lady, I have a proposal too: if I guess your real hair color, can I have my dog back?"

51.

Q: What has an IQ of 50 and is 4 miles long?

A: A parade of blondes.

52.

Q: How did the blonde girl who said she was going to drink some milk die?

A: The cow fell on top of her.

53.

Three blonde girls step into a car to go on a road trip. After a few hours, their car breaks down, in the desert. They forgot to bring their phones, so they are not able to call anyone for help.

After some discussion, they agree that their best bet is to walk to the nearest city, about 10 miles away.

To make the journey a bit easier, they decide that they will all take one thing from the car with them.

The first blonde girl takes out the radio and says, "The walk is quite long, we'll probably get bored. If that happens, I'll turn on the radio and we can listen to some country music."

The second blonde looks at the car and then takes one of the wheels. She says: "I'm not sure if we're going to make it to town walking. If not, we can all go inside the wheel and roll to town."

Finally, the third blonde, after considering her options, decides to take the car door. She says: "We're in the desert, in the blazing sun. If it gets too hot, I will roll down the window!"

54.

One day, a traveling blonde sat next to a lawyer on an airplane. The lawyer insisted on playing a game of intelligence. Finally, she gave in, when the lawyer offered her really good odds: 10 to 1. She would owe him $10 for each question she could not answer, whereas he would give her $100 for each question he could not answer. The lawyer figured there'd be no way he would lose this game.

The lawyer's first question was: "What is the distance between London and Paris?" The blonde immediately gave him $10, without even saying a word.

Then it was the blonde's turn. She asked, "What goes up a mountain with 3 legs and comes back down with 4 legs?"

That was a tough one, the lawyer was puzzled. He spent several hours, even using the Wi-Fi on the airplane to find the answer. Finally, very frustrated, he gave up: "Here's your $100."

Without comment, the blonde girl put the $100 into her pocket. Then the lawyer asked, "So, what is the answer?"

Without saying anything, the blonde gave him another $10.

55.

One day, a blonde's neighbor's house caught fire. She was the first to notice, so she dialed 911.

She told the operator, "Come quickly, the house of my neighbor is on fire!" The operator asked, "Tell me where you are" To which the blonde replied, "I'm at home."

The operator responded, "No, that's not what I mean: I want to know how to get there?"

To which the blonde replied, "Don't play games with me: in a fire truck, of course!"

56.

Q: Why do blondes take a ruler to bed?

A: Because they want to measure how long they sleep.

57.

At the doctor's office, a blonde hears she is pregnant with twins. When she hears the news, she starts crying. The doctor asks: "What's the matter?"

The blonde replies, "Well, I know my husband is the father of one of the babies. But I don't know who fathered the other one! How am I going to tell my husband?"

58.

A blonde was so fed up with all the blonde jokes that she decided to take drastic measures: she wanted to hang herself in the bathroom. After locking the bathroom door, she shouted at her husband, "I'm going to hang myself because I can't take any more of these dumb blonde jokes!"

Her husband, in panic, kicked in the bathroom door. Then he saw her his blonde wife with a rope tied on her ring finger. The husband said, "What's this: I thought you said you were going to hang yourself." She replied, "Yes, I totally am!" Her husband responded, "Well, sweetie, usually people tie the rope around their neck when they try to hang themselves. Why did you tie the rope to your ring finger?" Then the blonde said, "I started with that, but I couldn't breathe."

59.

A fat brunette, a skinny redhead, and a blonde are walking in the desert when they find a magic mirror. If you look into this mirror and lie, you die immediately.

The brunette looks into the mirror and says: "I look so thin", and dies on the spot. Then, the redhead looks into the mirror and says, "I look so fat," and also dies. Next, the blonde looks in the mirror and says, "I think..." and drops dead.

60.

In a suburb, a man was mowing the grass in his front yard, when his attractive blonde neighbor walked out of her house and walked straight to the mailbox. He saw her opening it, then slamming it shut and storming back into her house.

A little later, the blonde came out again, marched to the mailbox and opened it, only to slam it shut again seconds later. Clearly upset, she walked back into her house.

As the man was still puzzled about what was going on, she came out a third time. Again, she opened the mailbox and then slammed it shut as hard as she could.

Finally, the man asked the blonde "Howdy neighbor, is something the matter?"

To which she responded, "Yes!" My stupid laptop keeps saying, "You've got mail!"

61.

A man sits down in a restaurant. "May I take your order?" the blonde waitress asks him.

"Yes please, can you tell me how you prepare your chickens?"

"Oh, nothing special, sir," she responded, "we are pretty direct: we simply tell them they're going to die."

62.

A blonde desperately needed some extra money. She came up with the brilliant idea of kidnapping a child and holding him for ransom. So, she went to the local playground, grabbed a little boy, took him two blocks away from the playground, and said to him, "Don't make a wrong move, I have kidnapped you."

Next, she took a big piece of paper and wrote the following on it, "I have kidnapped your boy. To get him back, put $5,000 in an envelope tomorrow evening and leave it under the oak tree next to the bridge. Signed, a blonde."

Then, the blonde pinned the note to the boy's shirt, told him, "Show this to your parents", and sent him home.

The next evening, the blonde went to the oak tree next to the bridge, and sure enough, there was an envelope beneath it.

She opened the envelope and found the $5,000 she asked for. There was also a note in there that said, "Shame on you, how can you do this to a fellow blonde?"

63.

Q: What do blondes do when they hear that 80% of car accidents occur around the house?

A: They move.

64.

Q: What happens when a blonde is diagnosed with Alzheimer's disease?

A: Her IQ increases!

65.

A blonde goes to see a nutritionist, because she's obese. The nutritionist tells her "Here's what I want you to do. Eat regularly for 2 days, then skip 1 day. Repeat this for 2 weeks and you will lose at least 6 pounds."

Two weeks later, the blonde returns to the office. When she steps on the scale, the nutritionists see that she has lost a whopping 20 pounds.

The nutritionist is baffled, "That's insane! Did you follow the diet I gave you?"

The blonde replies, "Yes, but I thought I was going to die every 3rd day from all the skipping you made me do!"

66.

A brunette, a redhead, and a blonde all work at the same advertisement agency for a female boss who always leaves the office early. One day, the redhead tells the other girls, "Why don't we also leave home early today? The boss will never know!"

So, that afternoon, the three of them leave right after the boss does. The redhead goes shopping. The brunette gets a good work-out at the gym. When the blonde goes home, she finds her boyfriend having sex with her boss! She tiptoes out of the house and returns a few hours later, at her normal time.

"That was great," the redhead says the very next day, "Let's do that again sometime!" "I'm out," the blonde replies "I almost got caught!"

67.

One day, I got a phone call from a blonde I met in the bar, and she said, "Hey, can you tell me your phone number again? I can't find it anywhere!"

68.

It is one of those days again where a blonde decides enough is enough: "I'm sick of all these stupid blonde jokes!" She feels it's time to take a stand, and show her husband that she's actually really intelligent. She decides that she will paint a few rooms on the house, while her husband is at the office. She gets started the very next day.

The next day, her husband arrives home at 6pm. As he opens the door, the distinctive smell of paint enters his nostrils. As he walks into the living room, he is shocked: there's his wife, lying on the floor, in a pool of sweat. What's even more strange is that she is wearing a fur coat and a winter jacket at the same time.

He leans over her and asks: "Are you OK, honey?". When she responds that she is, he continues "What on earth are you doing?"

She replies, "I wanted to paint the house, to show you that not all blondes are stupid."

"That's very sweet,", the man replies, "but why then are you wearing a fur coat over a winter jacket?"

"Well," she replied, "The directions on the paint cans said 'For best results, <u>put on 2 coats</u>.'"

69.

Q: Why do blondes like lightning so much?

A: Because they think someone is taking a picture of them.

70.

One day, a blonde woman is wearing a pair of socks to work that don't match. One sock is blue, the other sock is green.

Her colleague notices it, and says, "Do you know that your socks do not match? One is blue, the other one is green."

The blonde replies, "That is so strange! Would you believe me if I tell you that I have an identical pair in my drawer at home?"

71.

Man, at a job interview: "Tell me where you were born."

Blonde woman: "In the United States."

Man: "Which part?"

Blonde woman: "My whole body."

72.

A brunette, a redhead, and a blonde are sitting in a bar. As they drink their Martini's, they start to ponder what they would do if they'd be able to go into space.

"I would go to Mars and cuddle a Martian," the brunette says.

The redhead says, "I would go to the Moon, so I can see the Earth in all its glory."

The blonde says, "I would go all the way to the sun."

The brunette replies, "But you would burn up and die if you would do that!" To which the blonde responded, "No, I thought about that. I will only fly at night."

73.

A redhead and a blonde are in a car, on a road trip. The redhead is driving, while the blonde is sitting in the passenger seat. As they are going down a steep hill, the redhead starts to panic when she realized that the brakes do not work.

"The brakes don't work!", she yells at the blonde, "We will drive off the cliff!"

The blonde remains calm though, and replies, "No need to worry! There's a stop sign ahead."

74.

A man and his blonde wife are trying to have a baby. Finally, after many tries, the blonde has good news.

She tells her husband, "Sweetie, sit down, I have amazing news! I am pregnant. And guess what: we are going to have twins!"

Her husband starts jumping up and down on the couch from excitement. When he calms down, he asks his wife: "Baby, this is great news indeed. But we haven't even seen a doctor: how do you know we are going to have twin babies?"

She replies, "When I went to the store, I bought the twin pack pregnancy test. I did the test and they both came out positive!"

75.

Q: How can you make a blonde girl laugh on Sunday?

A: Tell her a joke on Thursday.

76.

Two blonde women are walking downtown, when one of them notices a broken piece of mirror lying on the ground.

She picks it up, looks at it and says, "This woman looks very familiar. Who is it? I can't remember where I have seen her before."

Then, the other blonde looks into the mirror and says, "You're such an idiot. It's me!"

77.

A blonde walks up to a clerk in a computer store and asks, "Can you tell me where you keep the curtains for computers?" The clerk doesn't understand, so he replies "I'm sorry, what do you mean? Computers don't need curtains."

To which the blonde replies, shaking her head vigorously at so much incompetence, "Where did you get your education!? I have Windows on my computer!"

78.

A blonde woman gets lost in the city, so she calls her husband to ask for directions. Her husband picks up the phone, and asks: "Which cross streets are you at?".

To which the blonde responds, "I am standing on the corner of Walk and Do Not Walk."

79.

One evening, a redhead and a blonde have a girls' night and are watching a soap opera.

The redhead says: "I bet you $5 that Jimmy will jump off a building in this episode." The blonde takes her up on the bet and loses: Jimmy jumped off a building. So, the blonde pays the redhead $5.

An hour later, the redhead – feeling guilty – confesses: "Actually, I have already seen this episode. I knew he was going to jump."

To which the blonde replies, "I also have something to confess. I have seen this episode too, but I didn't think Jimmy would be stupid enough to jump again!"

80.

One day, a blonde was having a coffee with her best friend at Starbucks, and asker her, "I don't understand: my brother has two sisters. Why do I only have one?"

81.

Q: What do blonde women and dim lamps have in common?

A: Blonde women and dim lamps both tend to be hot, but not too bright.

82.

After a hard day of work, a blonde woman leaves the office, only to see her car being stolen right in front of her.

When the police officers arrived, they asked her: "Were you able to see the guy who stole your car?" The blonde replied, "No, unfortunately I wasn't. But...I got the license plate!"

83.

A policeman is doing his round when he sports a blonde woman driving her car and knitting at the same time. As he drives up next to her, he opens the window and yells at her, "Pull over!"

The blonde woman looks to the left, rolls down her window, and says, "No fluffhead, it's a scarf!"

84.

Q: Why did the blonde girl stare at the orange juice box in the supermarket?

A: Because the orange juice box said, "Concentrate."

85.

Q: How would you drown a blonde woman in a submarine?

A: Just knock on the door.

86.

After he has seen a few other patients, a blonde steps into the doctor's office. "What can I do for you?", he asks.

"Well, every time I drink my coffee my eye starts to hurt," the blonde said.

That is strange, the doctor thought to himself. So he called his assistant to bring in a cup of coffee from the machine in the kitchen.

As the doctor watched, the blonde took a sip from the cup. Sure enough, she yelled: "Ow! That really hurts!"

She put the cup down, when the doctor said, "I know what the problem is."

"Just tell it to me straight, doc," the blonde replied, "How bad is it?"

The doctor responded, "It is very simple: all you need to do is take the spoon out of your cup before you take a sip of your coffee."

87.

A man is waiting in line for a soda machine. At the front of the line is a blonde woman, who puts in a dollar to get her drink. But then she puts in another dollar, to get another soda. And another dollar...

The man asks: "Hey, what's taking so long?"

The blonde replies, "Shush, can't you see I'm winning here?"

88.

A blonde woman walked up to the librarian, and slammed the book she wanted to return on the table, "This book is absolutely terrible, you know that? It has a crazy amount of characters. Also, the plot makes no sense whatsoever!"

The librarian replied, "Thank you for returning our phone book. We weren't able to find it."

89.

Two blondes went shopping. They ended their shopping day by going to the movies. When they left the cinema and walked to their car on the parking lot, a beautiful Ford Mustang convertible, they realized the keys were still inside the car.

They just stood there for a while, not sure what to do. Then, one blonde said: "Wait, I got a coat hanger with one of my new dresses. Let's try to open the car with it." So she took it out, and began to fiddle with the lock.

As she was trying, the other blonde noticed the sky was getting darker and darker, and she started to worry. "Come on, girl, hurry up! It's looks like it is about to rain any second, and we left the top down!"

90.

Q: What would you call a skeleton found in the closet?

A: The 1872 Blonde Hide-and-Seek champion!

91.

Q: What is the best way to confuse a blonde woman?

A: Give her a box of cereal and tell her: "Here, solve this jigsaw puzzle."

92.

After dreaming about it for years, a blonde finally decides today is the day: I'm going to ride a horse!

On her first ride, she loses control. As she falls of the horse, her foot gets stuck in the stirrup, so she falls on her head.

Just as she is about to lose consciousness, the carny stops the carousel.

93.

Two blondes are on opposite sides of the river. One blonde shouts to the other blonde, "Hey, can you tell me how to get to the other side of the river?"

To which the other blonde replied, "Silly, you *are* on the other side!"

94.

A man walks on the street when he is
approached by a blonde. She asks him:
"Excuse me, sir, can you tell me what time it is?"
The man says, "Sure, it's 10:26."

The blonde replies, "Really? That is so strange.
I get a different answer each time I ask
someone that question..."

95.

Q: What are the first words a blonde says after she graduates college?

A: "Would you like to supersize that meal?"

96.

A blonde wanted to go shopping. So she drove to the shopping mall. In the parking lot, she found a parking spot with a sign next to it: '1 Hour Only.'

However, she wanted to go shopping for 2 hours. So she parked her car across 2 parking spaces.

97.

Q: What do a unicorn and an intelligent blonde have in common?

A: They are both fictional characters.

98.

Did you see that item on yesterday's news about those two blonde girls that froze to death at a drive-in cinema?

They went to see "Closed for the Winter."

99.

A man is driving in his car when he sees an attractive blonde walking down the street, with a big bag in her hand.

As he pulls up next to her, he asks, "Hello there, can I ask what you have in that bag?"

"Sure,", the blonde woman says, "'I have chickens in here!"

Then, the man says, "I have a proposal for you: If I can guess how many chickens you have in there, can I keep one?"

The blonde thinks it over for a moment, and then agrees. "OK," she replies, "but I'd like to up the ante! If you can guess exactly how many chickens I have in this bag, you can have BOTH of them!"

100.

Q: Why are there seventeen blonde girls waiting outside the club?

A: Because the sign says you need to be 18 to get in.

101.

A blonde girl is doing a puzzle, and asks her friend: "Help me out here, what is the second to last letter of the alphabet?"

Her friend says: "Y."

The blonde replies: "Because I am trying to solve this puzzle. Do you really have to question everything I say?!"

BONUS JOKES

These are <u>11 bonus jokes</u> from my popular book *'101 Hilarious Yo Mama Jokes.'*

Enjoy!

***

1.

Your momma is so poor, when she saw the garbage truck she went running after it with a grocery list.

2.

Your momma is so dumb, she went back to Dunkin' Donuts to return a donut because it had a hole in it!

3.

Your momma is so dumb, she once opened a bag of M&M's and tried to put them in alphabetical order.

4.

Your momma is so dumb, when thieves broke into her house and stole the coffee machine, she followed them outside and yelled to them, "Hey, you forgot the coffee!"

5.

Your momma is so fat, one day she saw a yellow school bus go by filled with white kids and she ran after it yelling, "TWINKIE!"

6.

Your momma is so dumb, she brought a spoon to watch the Super Bowl.

7.

Your momma is so fat, last Christmas I took a picture of her and it's still printing now.

8.

Your momma is so ugly, she forced One
Direction to go another direction.

9.

Your momma is so dumb, I saw her put two quarters in her ears and then she thought she was listening to a 50 Cent record.

10.

Your momma is so fat, this morning she stepped on the scale and it said, "I need your weight girl, not your phone number."

11.

Your momma is so dumb, when your family was driving in the car to Disneyland, she noticed a sign that said "Disneyland left," so she turned around to go home.

***

This is the end of this bonus chapter.

Want to continue reading?

Then get your copy of "101 Hilarious Yo Mama Jokes" at your favorite bookstore!

DID YOU LIKE THIS BOOK?

If you enjoyed this book, I would like to ask you for a favor. Would you be kind enough to share your thoughts and post a review of this book online? Just a few sentences would already be really helpful.

Your voice is important for this book to reach as many people as possible.

The more reviews this book gets, the more people will be able to find it and have a good laugh with these funny jokes!

***

IF YOU DID NOT LIKE THIS BOOK, THEN PLEASE TELL ME! You can email me at **feedback@semsoli.com**, to share with me what you did not like.

Perhaps I can change it.

A book does not have to be stagnant, in today's world. With feedback from readers like yourself, I can improve the book. So, you can impact the quality of this book, and I welcome your feedback. Help make this book better for everyone!

Thank you again for reading this book: I hope you had a good laugh!

OHTER BOOKS
BY
JOHNNY RIDDLE

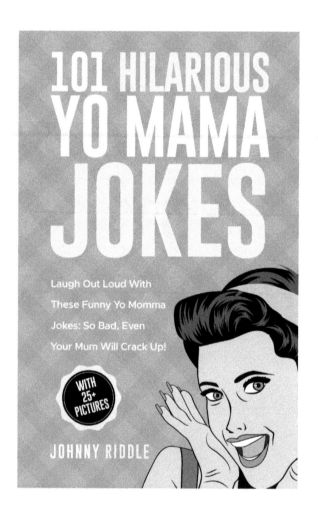

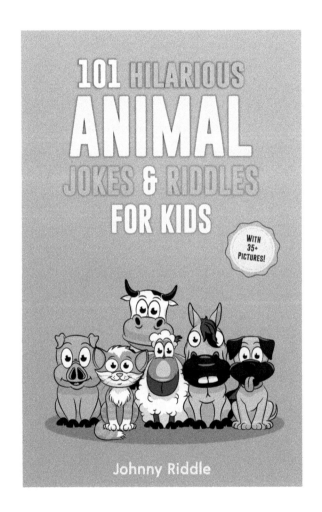

101 HILARIOUS ANIMAL JOKES & RIDDLES FOR KIDS

WITH 35+ PICTURES!

Johnny Riddle

101 HILARIOUS
CLEAN
JOKES & RIDDLES
FOR KIDS

WITH 30+ PICTURES!

Johnny Riddle